EMU ON THE LOOSE

By Dr. ZANYK

A Journey of Empowerment, Confidence & Freedom

Ordering Information:

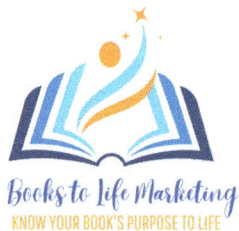

Books to Life Marketing
KNOW YOUR BOOK'S PURPOSE TO LIFE

Books to Life Marketing Ltd
128 City Road, London, EC1V 2NX, UK

Printed in the United States of America

Dedicated to
All the Adventurers Out There

One glorious morning on a fine summer day,
A young mother named Mimi called her children to play.
"Come, Julia, Nicholas, Noah and Leo"
It's time for a walk down the trail so, "Let's Go!"

Together they assembled, with their dog named Carley.
A Border Collie smart as a whip!
And settled their elderly orange pussycat, Bear.
into the stroller . . . to protect his sore hip.

Together they climbed the big hill to the trail, and walked happily for half an hour. Suddenly, Mimi glanced up and thought to herself,

"My eyes must be losing all power!"

From a distance, the image looked strange and quite blurry. She could tell it had feathers or was definitely furry. It looked like a two-legged horse on the loose or could it be a monster-sized Canada goose?

"No, no that's not it," Mimi squinted to focus. I know what that is and it's no hocus-pocus. That thing is an Emu, a huge flightless bird. Running loose on the trail? How very absurd!

Escaped from an Emu farm, 10 miles away. She'd been running round loose for one night and one day. Now blocked on the trail by steep cliffs on each side, with a mountain biker behind, there was nowhere to hide.

"We're going to have to catch her!" Mimi called to the biker.

"I agree" the biker called back. "I've already called the police on my cell phone that I carry inside my backpack!"

8

Mimi turned to her children with a stern look in her eyes. As she warned them, "this is serious, if you're scared . . . shut your eyes."
You must stay behind the stroller and do as I say.
These smart kids smelled danger and mumbled, "OK."

Now sheep herding was how Carley earned her keep. And boy, was she itching to chase this strange "sheep."
Bear on the other hand, in his 'cool cat' style, just yawned as he thought, "we'll be here for a while."

When suddenly, a white van drove onto the trail.
Out stumbled two people looking tired and pale.
A man and a woman with exhausted looking faces,
Frisco and Freya from O'Malley's Emu Oasis.

These two farmers grabbed their lassos and approached
the small crowd.
In a voice that was gruff and excessively loud,
Ms. O'Malley warned Mimi, "Beware of its front kick!"
"Cuz it's powerful, dangerous, and surprisingly quick."

The farmers then awkwardly moved in slow motion.
While Mimi and her kids giggled at the commotion.
Each time their lassos missed the neck of this bird,
The bird looked cleverer, and they looked absurd.

Mimi watched in amusement wondering, "who are they kidding?"
They'll never catch this bird, and I am tired of sitting.
"I'll catch this feisty bird, just give me a lasso!"
And that is exactly what she intended to do.

Except, that the Emu really hated that noose
that O'Malley was throwing and so... she broke loose.
Pushed right past Miss Mountain Bike and bolted down the trail.
Like a convict running for freedom, after breaking out of jail.

Mimi turned to Carley . . . they both understood.
They both knew her sheep herding skills were good.
"Ok Girl, you're up!" Mimi called, "Away to me."
And Carley performed a long out run with glee.

To a dog, this was better than boring old sheep.
And Carley could herd those old sheep in her sleep.
But this animal was different; it looked very appealing.
With its long legs and neck reaching up to the ceiling.

Carley pushed herself hard and ran past the Emu.
Then forced it to walk back, just as she was meant to.
Everyone was fascinated by this 'Canine machine.'
And didn't notice the Sheriff had arrived on the scene.

His name was Big Bob, and he was big, bald, and burly.
His hat covered a head that had lost its hair early.
He was thinking, "this call to catch an Emu confirms what
they say, my job as a sheriff doesn't earn enough pay!"

Lucky for him that brave Mimi was there.
She took control of the scene, without messing her hair.
Calling out commands to the people around, when,
suddenly
The Emu lost footing and stumbled to the ground.

"Now's our chance!" Mimi called, without missing a beat.
She grasped the Emu's neck as it got to its feet.
Aware of the danger in pulling this stunt,
Mimi remembered the story of a Cassowary - manhunt.

Cassowaries live in the rainforests of Australia. They're adorned with the strangest looking regalia. Shaggy feathers sprout a neck, and boney helmeted head.

With claws like bananas and STRENGTH . . . it is said . . . That can rip a man open; leave him to die, rarely live. And that's the story Mimi remembered about this Emu relative.

The tale of a jogger whose "thumping" of his feet. Served as a threatening call to action; to attack and defeat.

The Cassowary jumped into his powerful high kick.
Using daggerlike claws, it was over so quick.
The man fell victim to lightning speed and incredible power,
Ripped open, he fell and lived his last hour.

Mimi maintained her grip, jumping quickly to one side.
When the Emu started kicking like a wild windmill ride.
Those clawed feet propelled 'round with unbelievable power,
If Mimi got in their way, it would be her darkest hour.

In the chaotic flurry, rope might've done the trick.
Freya O'Malley tried roping legs but endured a strong kick,
that sent her flying frantically four feet in the air.
Before landing hard, she said an empty prayer.

Then, Mimi grabbed the rope and knew just what to do,
From watching a cowboy movie or two.
She performed a tidy rope trick like the 'best of the best.'
And that crowd, who was watching, was very impressed!

"Who… Are… You?" asked the sheriff, in awe and surprise.
"Wow!" gasped the farmers, their eyes big as pies.
"My name is Mimi," she politely replied.
Smiling back at her children, who were giggling with pride.

As Mimi was calming her excited four children,
O'Malley and Sheriff Bob lifted the Emu like 'strong men.'
After placing her safely in the back of the van,
Sheriff Bob suggested, "Loosen the ropes, just a bit, if you can."

"She'll ride more comfortably back to the farm."
O'Malley agreed, it would do no harm.
Now, poor tired out Emu lay perfectly still.
Till O'Malley slammed the door then... with all her will,

Flung off those old ropes and jumped to her feet.
Then flipped her awkward body over the big backseat.
She wiggled and rolled and with all her might,
Flipped over the driver seat, landing up right!

What lay before her was the best kind of surprise.
Our Emu just couldn't believe her own eyes.
There were buttons and baubles and doodads galore.
She bit down on a button and locked all the doors.

She proceeded to PECK, TASTE, NIBBLE and PLAY,
Then glanced at something that took her breath away.
Some keys had been forgotten in the ignition.
And were sparkling in the sun like a heavenly vision.

Those keys looked so shiny and delicious as well.
Emu pecked them so hard, her beak started to swell.
She tightened her grip, twisted her head and no lie . . .
The engine started up on the very first try.

The crowd was dumbfounded at this incredible feat.
The Emu was now sitting in the driver seat!
Their jaws hung open as the scene was so stunning.
Most shocking was the fact that the engine was running!

Sheriff Bob tried the doors, but it was no use.
Our Emu, once again, was "Emu on the Loose".
How quickly she adapted, to use her strong beak,
To give the gearshift handle an effective tweak.

The van slipped from Park into Drive; oh, it was sweet!
As she controlled the gas and steering wheel with her big
clunky feet. The ultimate moment of that whole crazy day,
was the moment that Emu simply drove away.

There were news reports, I don't know if they're true;
of a long necked hairy person at the McDonald's Drive-Thru.
But being unable to speak the words, Big Mac and Fries.
She got no food service, despite several tries.

Alas, tired and still hungry for a burger and fries,
Our Emu drove back to her farm.
She told her farm friends of her escapades,
who were glad she made it home without harm.

She gobbled a huge bowl of extra sweet grain,
Only the best would do,
Then, flopped into her bed for a much-deserved rest
That's what I'd do... Wouldn't you?